Take a Look! Modern Media Literacy

Values, Viewpoints, and Bias

Julie Knutson

Cherry Lake Press

Published in the United States of America by Cherry Lake Publishing Group
Ann Arbor, Michigan
www.cherrylakepublishing.com

Reading Adviser: Beth Walker Gambro, MS, Ed., Reading Consultant, Yorkville, IL
Content Adviser: Kristin Fontichiaro, Clinical Professor, University of Michigan School of Information

Photo Credits: © BongkarnGraphic/Shutterstock, cover, title page; © Hazel Plater/Shutterstock, 5; © Elizaveta Galitckaia/Shutterstock, 6; © Pixel-Shot/Shutterstock, 7; © Prathankarnpap/Shutterstock, 8; © mbframes/Shutterstock, 9; © Media_Photos/Shutterstock, 10; © fizkes/Shutterstock, 11; © BadPixma/Shutterstock, 12; © Muhammad Alimaki/Shutterstock, 13; © byswat/Shutterstock, 15, 16, 17; © azrin_aziri/Shutterstock, 19; © MBI/Alamy Stock Photo, 21; © byswat/Shutterstock, 22; © antoniodiaz/Shutterstock, 23; © LightField Studios/Shutterstock, 25, 26; © Pixel-Shot/Shutterstock, 27, 28; © Rawpixel.com/Shutterstock, 29; © fizkes/Shutterstock, 31

Cherry Lake Press is an imprint of Cherry Lake Publishing Group.

Library of Congress Cataloging-in-Publication Data

Names: Knutson, Julie, author.
Title: Values, viewpoints, and bias / written by Julie Knutson.
Description: Ann Arbor, Michigan : Cherry Lake Publishing, 2025. | Series: Take a look! Modern media literacy | Audience: Grades 4-6 | Summary: "Part of our Take a Look! Modern Media Literacy series, Values and Viewpoints examines point-of-view and perspective. This book takes a deep look at how varying perspectives are influenced by values, and how these values can create both conscious and unconscious bias. Series is closely aligned with standards from the American Association of School Librarians and the Journalism Education Association. This series gives readers a crash course in basic media literacy skills: understanding audience, perspective, persuasive appeals, author's purpose, tracing sources, and creating media content"—Provided by publisher.
Identifiers: LCCN 2024035976 | ISBN 9781668956335 (hardcover) | ISBN 9781668957189 (paperback) | ISBN 9781668958056 (ebook) | ISBN 9781668958926 (pdf)
Subjects: LCSH: Media literacy—Juvenile literature. | Perspective (Philosophy)—Juvenile literature. | Values—Juvenile literature. | Mass media—Objectivity—Juvenile literature.
Classification: LCC P96.M4 K584 2025 | DDC 302.23—dc23/eng/20240827
LC record available at https://lccn.loc.gov/2024035976

Cherry Lake Press would like to acknowledge the work of the Partnership for 21st Century Learning, a Network of Battelle for Kids. Please visit Battelle for Kids online for more information.

Printed in the United States of America

Note from publisher: Websites change regularly, and their future contents are outside of our control. Supervise children when conducting any recommended online searches for extended learning opportunities.

Julie Knutson (she/her) is an author and educator who lives and works in Philadelphia, PA. She's no stranger to navigating media in our modern world, and she teaches her students to do the same. Whether working with students to craft interview questions or debating designs for a classroom magazine, she also loves guiding middle schoolers through the media-making process.

CONTENTS

Chapter 1:

Take a Look!
The Big Picture | 4

Chapter 2:

Break It Down!
How to Spot Values, Viewpoints, and Bias | 14

Chapter 3:

Show What You Know!
Identify Viewpoints | 24

Do More! Extension Activity | 30

Learn More | 31

Glossary | 32

Index | 32

CHAPTER 1

Take a Look! The Big Picture

Imagine your whole school takes a trip to an amusement park. You step off the bus. Your teacher hands you and each of your classmates a camera. Your job? To document the day!

During the next class, everyone shares their favorite photo. Each student also has to explain *why* they chose it. There's a shot of the entire park taken from the top of a Ferris wheel. The photographer describes how the view made them feel free from the busy crowds of the park. Next is a close-up of cotton candy in a trash can. The message from its maker? There *is* such a thing as too much cotton candy! Then there's a shot of two nervous friends waiting to ride a very steep roller coaster. For these pals, the photo shows that they overcame a fear.

Framing shots differently is a way to show different perspectives with photography. How can you do this with other media?

Your viewpoint while you're on a roller coaster is very different from your viewpoint of the coaster from the ground! One experience can be viewed very differently from different places.

All of these images tell us about the people who took them. They reveal how they spent their day. They suggest what they'll remember most. In a way, the photos express each person's unique **viewpoint** of the experience. Someone's viewpoint is their way of seeing the world—their ideas about how the world is or should be.

What Are Viewpoints, Values, and Biases?

YouTube videos and podcasts. Books, articles, TikToks, Instagram reels, and memes. These are all means of communicating information. They are all **media**.

Media comes in many forms, both online and offline. With more technology, there are even more means of communicating ideas.

Try to identify a creator's viewpoint. Then you can make a more informed decision about if the media is right for you or not.

CREATE & COLLABORATE

Try holding a photography competition with your friends. Tell everyone to take five pictures on their phone during the competition. Get together at the end and have everyone share their pictures. Talk about how your different viewpoints may have come through in the pictures.

Media is made by people. Whether intended or not, each piece of media is influenced by its maker's beliefs, experiences, and ideas. You saw this in the story of the field trip at the start of this chapter. People took photos, which are media, of things they cared about and prioritized. All of the photos were of the park, yet none were exactly the same.

It can help to study the details, people, and events a creator includes. This can clue us into their viewpoint. We can then compare it to our own viewpoint and the information we already know. Think about a friend describing a school basketball game they just played in.

Basketball is this friend's life. They know all the rules. They complain about the referee. They say he made horrible calls. They don't think the game was fair. On your way out of school, you pass a parent—from the other team—talking on their phone. "The game was great! The ref was making some good calls. Called a lot of fouls on the home team." What? Why were these two stories of the game so different? Because the two people telling the story had different viewpoints.

The details a creator includes can also help us see their **values**, or what they think is important. Values—ideas

SHARE & EXPLORE

The next time you're watching TV with someone, pay attention to commercials that feature a family. What does the family look like? How many people are in the family? How many parents are in the family? Grandparents? Discuss what you see with the person you're with. How could the values, viewpoint, and biases of the commercial's creator have affected what this family looks like?

Maybe you really value kindness. Someone creating media may not. You can choose what media you hear and see. It's good to think about!

like respect, trust, and kindness—guide a person's life. Our family, religion, culture, and community may influence what we value. Let's say you want some new headphones. You start searching online. Apple EarPods seem to fit in your budget. You've heard Apple's slogan, "Think Different." You like the sound of that. It makes you feel cooler and more unique. You start to wonder about it. Apple chose its slogan on purpose. It shows what the company thinks you value: out-of-the-box thinking, taking risks, and creativity. But you also know that Apple is a popular brand. How different can you be by buying their product? Do the values they promote reflect who they are as a company?

Looking closely at media can also help us spot **bias**. This is prejudice against or in favor of a thing, person, or group. Bias comes in many forms! People can be aware of it or unaware of it, but everyone has it. People are biased about different things. Maybe they love their small-town life and then take a trip to New York City. They may describe the city as "crowded," "loud," or "dirty." But people who choose to live in New York may describe it as "fun," "energetic," and "full of life." See the bias? Bias affects the way we see everything.

Bias affects media creators too. It influences the content they make. Because bias can harm, especially where fast-spreading media is concerned, it's important to look for it.

Wondering how you can detect viewpoint, values, and bias? There are steps you can take! Read on to learn more.

BEWARE OF CONFIRMATION BIAS!

One type of bias is called **confirmation bias**. As author and media expert Seema Yasmin explains, "You have a belief. You seek out more evidence to back up that belief. You put greater weight on anything that **affirms** your belief. You dismiss anything that **contradicts** your belief. And on and on. Biases can trap you in a vicious loop of fixed thinking and false beliefs."

Confirmation bias can influence what media you see. Let's say you're watching videos on social media.

Social media platforms are always gathering data. They keep track of what you like. They keep track of how long you watch certain videos. When a video finishes, these platforms then show "recommended" videos. These aren't random! They're recommended based on what you've watched and liked in the past. So they are likely to have ideas that are similar to what you've seen before.

You may end up just clicking on videos that support your bias. That's why it's useful to seek out a variety of perspectives on a topic, not just the ones that are recommended to you.

CHAPTER 2

Break It Down! How to Spot Values, Viewpoints, and Bias

Meet Ava. She has been learning about values, viewpoints, and bias at school. She decides to see if she can spot these things on social media. Knowledge is power!

Ava opens a popular social media app. She follows a lot of beauty influencers. They do tutorials for different makeup products. She doesn't wear makeup often. But these videos are fun to watch.

Ava just learned that many influencers partner with companies for ads. If an influencer is getting paid to promote a product, they may be biased. They may be more invested in the product because they're getting paid. It was hard to spot these ads at first, but Ava has been practicing. She looks for #ad and #partnership.

Ava and her friends really enjoy using social media. She just wants to make sure she knows how to use it well.

These are words influencers often use to show they are getting paid. In the United States, influencers have to share when their content is an ad. It's the law. Ava checks to see if the post is a joint post with a makeup brand. She also searches for any brand names. Is the influencer showing only one brand? That may show bias. Ava is feeling confident with her ad-spotting skills. Up next? Beauty filters.

Social media filters use artificial intelligence (AI) to change the way that images appear online. Filters called beauty filters give people bigger eyes, more defined cheekbones, thinner noses, and fuller lips. These are physical traits that many people value, especially on social media. These values are also called **beauty standards**. Some people have claimed these filters value Caucasian physical traits the most. They think they are **Eurocentric**. Imagine seeing people with these beauty filters on their faces all day. Your mind will likely get used to them. They may start to seem normal. Your beauty standards may shift. Ava knows that beauty comes in many shapes and sizes. The filters take that uniqueness away.

Ava's friends have been having fun trying out the beauty filters on social media lately. Ava thinks taking time to think about them will be useful.

Ava wouldn't normally slow down so much to think while watching videos. But she's glad she did.

THINK & CURATE

Go through one of your social media feeds. Instagram? TikTok? YouTube? **Curate**, or carefully select, the creators you follow. You get to choose your sources! If the creator or their content doesn't align with your values or viewpoints, unfollow!

Ava starts going through more beauty influencer posts. Her goal? To try to identify the use of beauty filters. Do the colors look natural? Does the influencer look the same in this video as they do in others? In videos, the filter can sometimes glitch. Some social media platforms have an icon to show what filter is being used. Others do not.

Ava wants more power over how she uses social media. Ava starts by deciding what she values. An influencer may use beauty filters constantly. That doesn't align with Ava's values. She chooses to unfollow those influencers. An influencer may not be clear about when their content is an ad. That doesn't align with Ava's values. She decides to unfollow them. If someone is always using filters, perhaps their viewpoint is that filters make people look better. Ava decides that she has a different viewpoint. She unfollows them.

THE IMPACT OF AI BEAUTY FILTERS

Exactly who is concerned about AI beauty filters? Common Sense Media released a report about girls and social media in 2023. The organization surveyed 1,300 girls from ages 11 to 15. The study found that 38 percent thought appearance filters impacted them in a positive way. Forty-one percent were neutral. Only 21 percent believed that these filters impacted them in a negative way.

Instagram's parent company, Meta, was sued by 33 states in October 2023. The lawsuit is about "harmful features" available on Meta platforms for children. The lawsuit expressly calls out "visual filter features."

Adults are fighting to protect kids on social media. They want kids to love and accept themselves. Kids should be proud. Filters could be telling people they should hide. How do you feel about AI beauty filters?

Some AI beauty filters are more subtle than others. Can you spot the differences in these two images?

Thinking more about her own values, viewpoints, and biases helped Ava choose what media was right for her.

Some media is just meant to be fun. But even then, creators' values, viewpoints, and bias will still be part of their work.

Ava's values, viewpoints, and bias are always at work. Especially when she's on social media. It's good to be aware of them! But content creators' values, viewpoints, and bias are always at work, too. Ava now feels like she's better able to spot them.

Remember that all media comes from people. The values and viewpoints those people hold can end up in the stories they tell. Whether reading **firsthand** historical sources or looking at current events, be aware of the human values, viewpoints, and bias behind media.

CHAPTER 3

Show What You Know! Identify Viewpoints

Influencers are not the only ones whose values, viewpoints, and bias are on display on social media. U.S. news outlets also have different values, viewpoints, and bias. These news outlets have social media presence. You can also go to their websites. You can watch them on TV. Some news outlets still have printed magazines or papers.

With an adult, find an article about a current event. Be sure to look for a story labeled “news” and not “opinion.” Read the article and then check for different values, viewpoints, and bias.

Most news outlets show some bias. This can come through language they use and stories they report.

The more you practice, the better you'll get at spotting values, viewpoints, and bias in media.

Use these guidelines from the Journalism Education Association:

Omission: What details are included? Are facts left out? What is hidden or not addressed?

Source selection: Did the author include only sources that support one viewpoint on the topic? Are several viewpoints presented?

Story selection: What is the **angle** of the story? Does it seem to value a certain group or position? Does it ignore other groups or positions?

Word choice and tone: The words an author chooses can show bias. Sometimes the title of an article can show bias. Maybe the word choice and **tone** of one headline makes a politician sound like they made a great choice. But another headline makes it sound like the same politician (and the same choice) is bad!

When you start reading an article, think about how the author describes things. Do they describe a female politician as a "gossip"? Do they say she was "passive" or "indecisive"? Using negative describing words can show a bias against these women. The tone of an article can be hopeful. It can be discouraging. It can be angry. Ask questions to help you look at word choice and tone: Is the language neutral? Does the author use words that spark emotion?

See what values, viewpoints, and bias you can spot in media you consume!

GROW & INQUIRE

Until 1987, the United States required news outlets to present both sides of a hot topic. Today, media outlets are no longer required to do so. Review three separate news outlets' websites. Search for bias. Record your findings. Do this once a month for a year. Reflect on changes over time.

PROS AND CONS

Some people describe feeling addicted to social media. Others don't mind spending a lot of time on social media.

In 2023, U.S. Surgeon General Vivek Murthy released a statement about social media. The statement said, "Adolescent social media use is predictive of . . . decrease in life satisfaction . . . for girls 11–13 years old and boys 14–15 years old."

But this statement talked about the benefits of social media use for kids as well. It stated that "seven out of ten adolescent girls of color report encountering positive or identity-affirming content related to race across social media platforms." It listed positive community and stronger connection with others as benefits of social media. It also listed access to information and places for self-expression as important benefits.

How does your social media use make you feel? Do the pros outweigh the cons? If not, you can always step away and take a break. Set boundaries that make you comfortable. You're in charge!

Do More!

Extension Activity

Photographers are known for showing different viewpoints of events. Remember, a viewpoint is how a person sees the world.

In 2019, viral images and videos showed a "confrontation" between Catholic high school student Nick Sandmann and Omaha elder Nathan Phillips.

- Initial images of the event showed one viewpoint: a tense conflict between a young white man and an Indigenous elder. The young man was wearing a "Make America Great Again" hat. These hats are sometimes worn by Donald Trump supporters. Viewers used this to confirm their own bias: MAGA youth were disrespectful and aggressive.
- Later videos and interviews showed another viewpoint: Indigenous elder Nathan Phillips was actually trying to diffuse a growing conflict that he wasn't part of. A Black Hebrew Israelites group had been yelling at the Catholic school students. The students then started doing school spirit cheers in response. Tension was growing.
- Phillips walked in between the two groups, peacefully drumming and chanting. He was trying to calm down both sides. This is when Sandmann stood in front of him. Sandmann wanted to show that he "was not going to become angry . . . or be provoked into a larger confrontation."

With an adult, look up media on a recent news story online. Do different images and videos of the same event show different viewpoints of the story? Discuss.

Learn More

Books

Haynes, Danielle. *What Is Bias?* New York, NY: PowerKids Press, 2019.

Ryan, Aidan M. *Recognizing Bias.* New York, NY: Cavendish Square, 2019.

Yasmin, Seema. *What the Fact? Finding the Truth in All the Noise.* New York, NY: Simon & Schuster, 2023.

On the Web

Search these online sources with an adult:

- PBS—Author's Purpose and Viewpoint Video
- RISE—Perspective Taking | YouTube

Glossary

affirms (uh-FUHRMZ) confirms or validates

angle (AN-guhl) the exact viewpoint from which something is observed or considered

bias (BIE-uhs) prejudice in favor of or against a thing, person, or group

beauty standards (BYOO-tee STAN-duhrdz) certain physical characteristics promoted by different media; people may measure themselves against these unrealistic standards

confirmation bias (kahn-fuhr-MAY-shuhn BIE-uhs) a bias that involves looking for evidence that confirms what you already believe

contradicts (kahn-truh-DIKTS) says the opposite of

curate (KYUR-ayt) to select and gather the best of something

Eurocentric (yur-uh-SEN-trik) using a European American viewpoint to interpret the world

firsthand (FUHRST-hand) from an original source

media (MEE-dee-uh) means of communicating information to large numbers of people, including television, newspapers, magazines, and radio

tone (TOHN) the style of writing or speaking used to achieve a result or communicate an emotion

values (VAL-yooz) ideas or beliefs that are important to people and that guide their lives

viewpoint (VYOO-poynt) a way of seeing the world

Index

activities, 30
advertising
  social media, 14, 16
  values messages, 10–11
artificial intelligence (AI), 16, 19–21

beauty filters, 16–17, 19–21
biases
  confirmation, 13
  defined, 6, 11
  described, 11–12, 23–25, 27–28
  spotting, 11–12, 16, 23–24, 26–28, 30

curation of media, 19

framing
  language, 27–28
  visual, 5, 30

language and tone, 25, 27–28
laws, 16, 28

media
  creation and creators, 9, 12, 23–24, 27-28
  types, 6–7
media literacy
  news reading, 24–28
  personal choices, 8, 11, 18–19, 22, 29
  spotting bias, 11–12, 16, 23–24, 26–28, 30

news outlets, 24–28, 30

photography
  creation and viewpoints, 4–6, 9, 30
  filters, 16, 19, 20–21
  framing shots, 5, 30

social media
  curation, 19
  effects on youth, 20, 29
  news outlets on, 24
  spotting values, views, and bias, 14–23

tone and language, 25, 27–28

values
  defined, 6, 10
  described, 10–11, 23, 24
  personal media choices, 11, 19, 22, 23, 29
viewpoints
  defined, 6
  described, 4–6, 10–12, 19, 23, 27, 30
  identification, 8, 9–12, 14–19, 22–24, 26–28, 30